MW01259731

# SUNDAY MORNING ORGANIST

*Alfred's Classic Editions*

This edition of the *Sunday Morning Organist* features unique introductions for familiar hymns and carols. Three experienced organ arrangers—Rebecca Kleintop Owens, Mark Thewes, and Jerry Westenkuehler—have combined their talents to provide today's church organist with innovative arrangements in a variety of musical styles. These inventive introductions will inspire the members of your congregation to enter into singing with confidence and enthusiasm.

## TABLE OF CONTENTS

Alfred Music Publishing Co., Inc.
P.O. Box 10003
Van Nuys, CA 91410-0003
alfred.com

ISBN-10: 0-7390-6528-9
ISBN-13: 978-0-7390-6528-0

Cover Image: © istockphoto.com/2windspa

# A MIGHTY FORTRESS IS OUR GOD

Martin Luther
Arranged by Rebecca K. Owens

# ALL CREATURES OF OUR GOD AND KING

*Geistliche Krichengesäng*
Arranged by Rebecca K. Owens

# ALL CREATURES OF OUR GOD AND KING

SW:   Full with Reeds
GT:   Full with Reeds, Sw. to Gt.
PED:  Full with Reeds, Sw. & Gt. to Ped.

*Geistliche Krichengesäng*
Arranged by Jerry Westenkuehler

**Majestically**

# ALL CREATURES OF OUR GOD AND KING

*Geistliche Krichengesäng*
Arranged by Mark Thewes

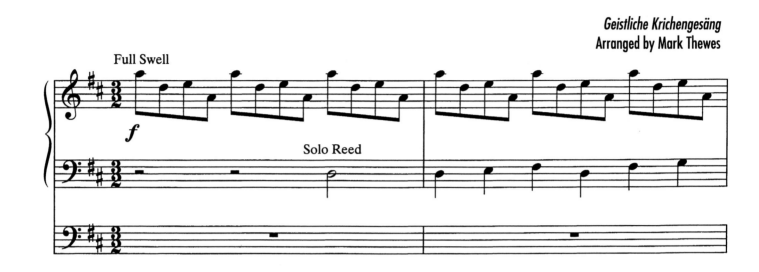

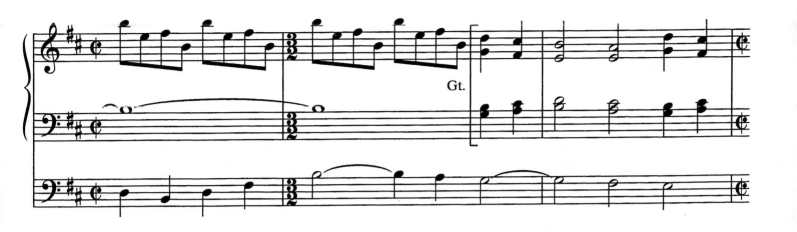

# ALL GLORY, LAUD, AND HONOR

Melchior Teschner
Arranged by Rebecca K. Owens

# ALL GLORY, LAUD, AND HONOR

SW:  Full with Reeds
GT:  Full with Reeds, Sw. to Gt.
PED: Full, Sw. & Gt. to Ped.

Melchior Teschner
Arranged by Jerry Westenkuehler

off Reeds

*Hymn*

All glo - ry, laud, and...

# ALL HAIL THE POWER OF JESUS' NAME

SW:    Full
GT:    Full, Bright Trumpet 8', Sw. to Gt.
PED:   Full, Sw. to Ped.

Oliver Holden
Arranged by Jerry Westenkuehler

# ALL HAIL THE POWER OF JESUS' NAME

Oliver Holden
Arranged by Rebecca K. Owens

# ANGELS WE HAVE HEARD ON HIGH

GT:  Full
PED:  Full

French Carol
Arranged by Jerry Westenkuehler

An - gels we have heard on high...

# ANGELS FROM THE REALMS OF GLORY

GT: Full
PED: Full

James Montgomery
Arranged by Jerry Westenkuehler

# CHRIST FOR THE WORLD WE SING

Italian Hymn
Arranged by Mark Thewes

# CHRIST THE LORD IS RISEN TODAY

SW: Full with Reeds
GT: Full with Reeds, Sw. to Gt.
PED: Full, Sw. & Gt. to Ped.

*Lyrica Davidica*
Arranged by Jerry Westenkuehler

**Majestically**

# CHRIST THE LORD IS RISEN TODAY

*Lyrica Davidica*
**Arranged by Mark Thewes**

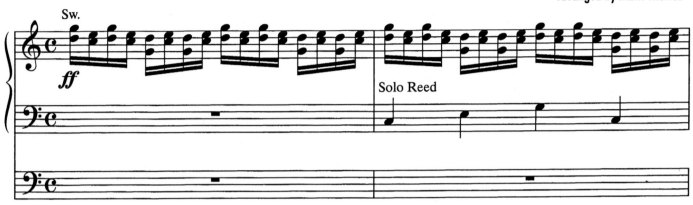

# COME, THOU ALMIGHTY KING

Felice De Giardini
Arranged by Rebecca K. Owens

Come, thou al -

# COME, THOU LONG-EXPECTED JESUS

Rowland H. Prichard
Arranged by Rebecca K. Owens

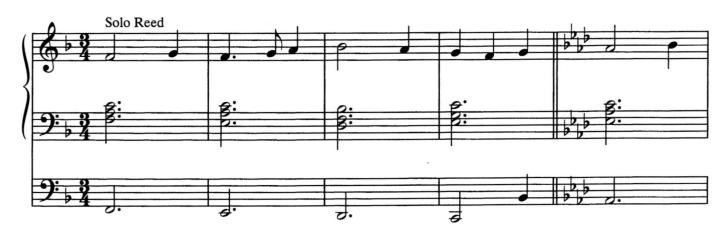

# CROWN HIM WITH MANY CROWNS

SW:  Full with Reeds
GT:   Full with Reeds, Sw. to Gt.
PED: Full, Sw. & Gt. to Ped.

George J. Elvey
Arranged by Jerry Westenkuehler

# CROWN HIM WITH MANY CROWNS

George J. Elvey
Arranged by Mark Thewes

# CROWN HIM WITH MANY CROWNS

George J. Elvey
Arranged by Rebecca K. Owens

# GO, TELL IT ON THE MOUNTAIN

GT: Full
PED: Full

Afro-American Spiritual
Arranged by Jerry Westenkuehler

Go tell it on the

# THE FIRST NOEL

SW: Flutes & Strings 8', 4'
GT: Principals 8', 4', 2', Sw. to Gt.
PED: Soft 16', Sw. to Ped.

Traditional English Carol
Arranged by Jerry Westenkuehler

# FOR THE BEAUTY OF THE EARTH

Conrad Kocher
Arranged by Mark Thewes

*To verse 1.  Interlude to Final verse*

*Last verse*

# THE GOD OF ABRAHAM PRAISE

GT: Full
PED: Full with Reeds

Hebrew melody
Arranged by Jerry Westenkuehler

off Ped. Reeds

The God of A - braham

# GOD OF GRACE AND GOD OF GLORY

SW:  Full
GT:  Full
PED:  Full

John Hughes
Arranged by Jerry Westenkuehler

# GOD OF GRACE AND GOD OF GLORY
## Setting No. 1

John Hughes
Arranged by Mark Thewes

# GOD OF GRACE AND GOD OF GLORY
## Setting No. 2

John Hughes
Arranged by Mark Thewes

# GOOD CHRISTIAN FRIENDS, REJOICE

GT:  Full
PED: Full

German carol
Arranged by Jerry Westenkuehler

Good Chris - tian friends, re - joice_____ with

# HARK! THE HERALD ANGELS SING

GT: Full
PED: Full

Felix Mendelssohn
Arranged by Jerry Westenkuehler

Hark! the her - ald an - gels sing

# HOLY, HOLY, HOLY! LORD GOD ALMIGHTY

GT: Principal 8', 4', 2', Mixture
PED: Full with Reeds 16', 8', Gt. to Ped.

John B. Dykes
Arranged by Jerry Westenkuehler

Hymn

Ho - ly, ho - ly,...

# HOLY, HOLY, HOLY! LORD GOD ALMIGHTY

Setting No. 2

John B. Dykes
Arranged by Rebecca K. Owens

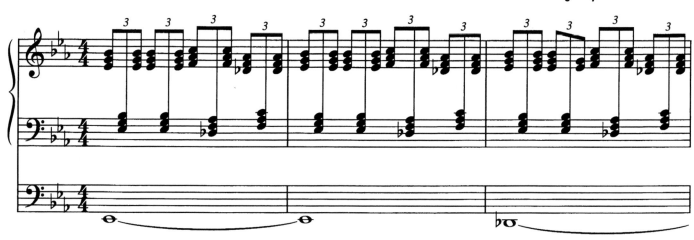

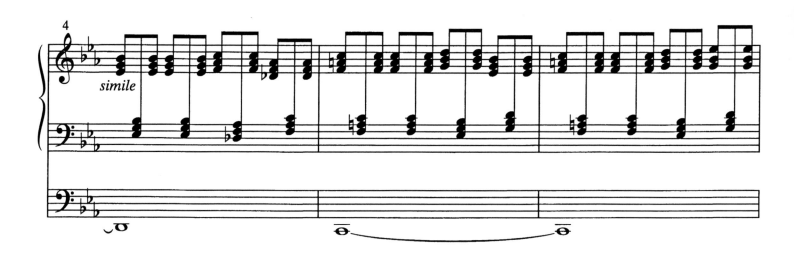

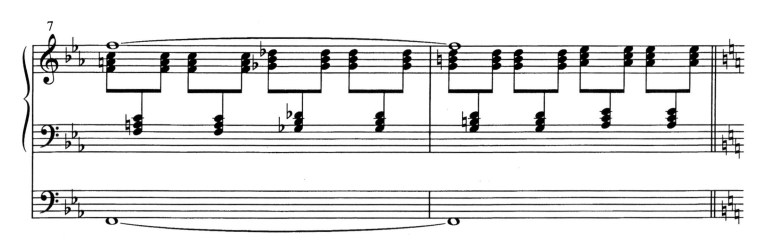

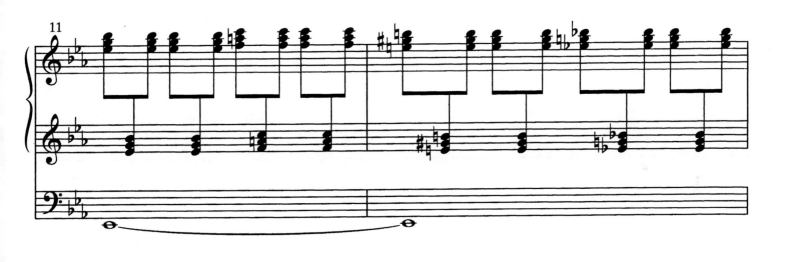

# HOLY, HOLY, HOLY! LORD GOD ALMIGHTY

### Setting No. 1

John B. Dykes
Arranged by Rebecca K. Owens

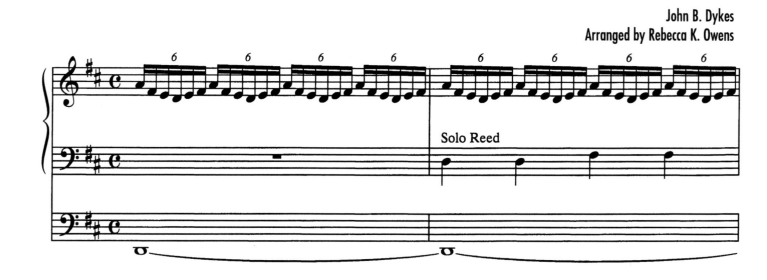

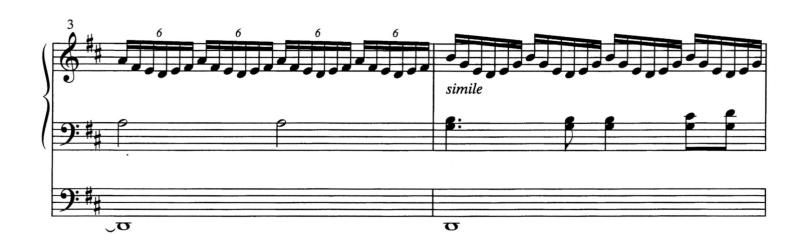

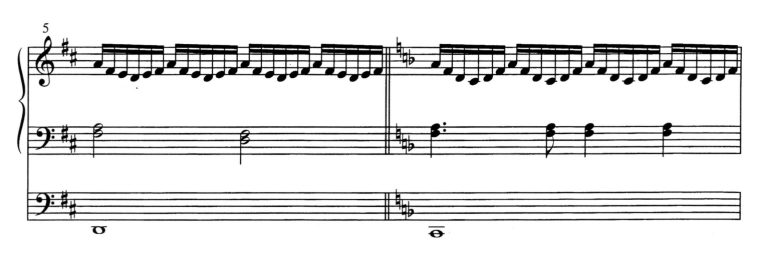

# HOW FIRM A FOUNDATION

Early American Melody
Arranged by Mark Thewes

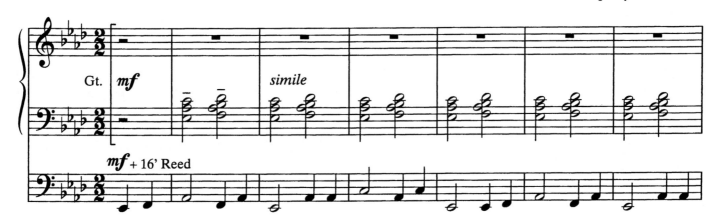

# HOW FIRM A FOUNDATION

GT:    Full
PED:   Full

Early American Melody
Arranged by Jerry Westenkuehler

How____ firm a foun -

# HOW FIRM A FOUNDATION

Early American Melody
Arranged by Rebecca K. Owens

# IT CAME UPON THE MIDNIGHT CLEAR

SW:  Solo Reed
GT:  Principals 8', 4', 2'
PED: 16', 8'

Richard Storrs Willis
Arranged by Jerry Westenkuehler

# IMMORTAL, INVISIBLE, GOD ONLY WISE

Traditional Welsh Melody
Arranged by Rebecca K. Owens

Solo Reed

Im - mor - tal, in -

# IMMORTAL, INVISIBLE, GOD ONLY WISE

GT:   Principals 8', 4', 2', Mixture
PED:  Principals 16', 8', Gt. to Ped.

Traditional Welsh Melody
Arranged by Rebecca K. Owens

# JESUS SHALL REIGN

John Hatton
Arranged by Rebecca K. Owens

Je - sus shall

# JOY TO THE WORLD!

SW: Chimes
GT: Full to Mixture
PED: Full

Issac Watts
Arranged by Jerry Westenkuehler

Joy to the

# JOYFUL, JOYFUL, WE ADORE THEE

SW:   Solo Trumpet
GT:   Full
PED:  Full

Ludwig van Beethoven
Arranged by Jerry Westenkuehler

# JOYFUL, JOYFUL, WE ADORE THEE

Ludwig van Beethoven
Arranged by Mark Thewes

# JOYFUL, JOYFUL, WE ADORE THEE

Ludwig van Beethoven
Arranged by Rebecca K. Owens

# LEAD ON, O KING ETERNAL

Henry T. Smart
Arranged by Rebecca K. Owens

# LEAD ON, O KING ETERNAL

SW:   Solo Trumpet 8'
GT:   Principals 8', 4', 2', Mixture
PED:  Full with Reeds 16', 8'

Henry T. Smart
Arranged by Jerry Westenkuehler

# LET US BREAK BREAD TOGETHER

GT:   Full
PED:  Full

*Afro-American Spiritual*
*Arranged by Jerry Westenkuehler*

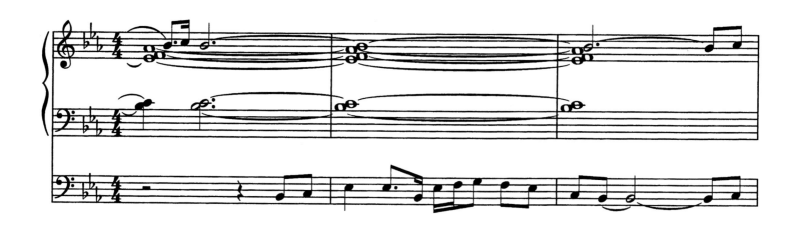

*Hymn*

Let us break bread to...

# LIFT HIGH THE CROSS

GT:   Full to Mixture
PED:   Full, Gt. to Ped.

Sydney Hugo Nicholson
Arranged by Jerry Westenkuehler

# LIFT HIGH THE CROSS

Sydney Hugo Nicholson
Arranged by Rebecca K. Owens

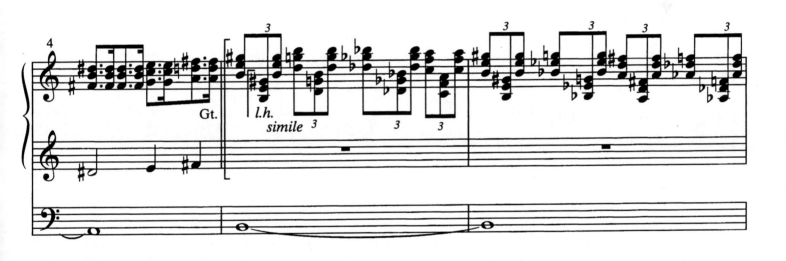

# LOVE DIVINE, ALL LOVES EXCELLING

John Zundel
Arranged by Rebecca K. Owens

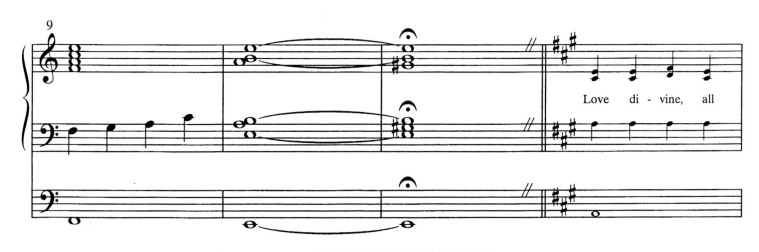

# MY COUNTRY, 'TIS OF THEE

*Thesaurus Musicus*
**Arranged by Mark Thewes**

# O COME, ALL YE FAITHFUL

GT: Full
PED: Full

John Francis Wade
Arranged by Jerry Westenkuehler

# O FOR A THOUSAND TONGUES TO SING

Carl G. Gläzer
**Arranged by Mark Thewes**

This setting can also be used for the last verse.

# O LITTLE TOWN OF BETHLEHEM

GT: Flutes & Strings 8', 4'
PED: Soft 16', Gt. to Ped.

Lewis H. Redner
Arranged by Jerry Westenkuehler

# O WORSHIP THE KING

Johann Michael Haydn
Arranged by Rebecca K. Owens

*This introduction also works with *Ye Servants of God* (Hanover), tune by William Croft

# O WORSHIP THE KING

SW: Full to Mixture
GT: Full, Trumpet 8', Sw. to Gt.
PED: Full, Sw. to Ped.

William Gardiner
Arranged by Jerry Westenkuehler

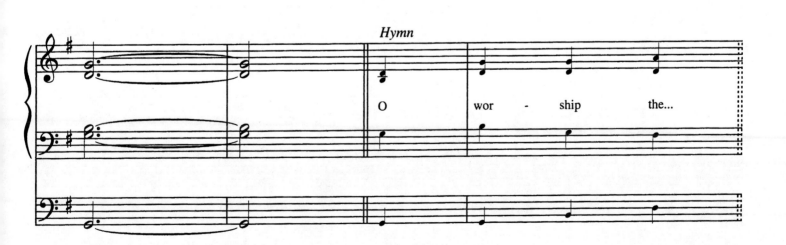

# ONCE IN ROYAL DAVID'S CITY

SW:  Solo Reed
GT:  Full
PED: Full

Henry J. Gauntlett
Arranged by Jerry Westenkuehler

Once in Roy - al Da - vid's_

# PRAISE, MY SOUL, THE KING OF HEAVEN

John Goss
Arranged by Rebecca K. Owens

*This introduction also works for the tune *Andrews*.

# PRAISE, MY SOUL, THE KING OF HEAVEN

SW:   Full
GT:   Full, Sw. to Gt.
PED: Full

John Goss
Arranged by Jerry Westenkuehler

Sw.　Gt.　Sw.

Gt.

Praise,　my　soul,　the　King　of

# PRAISE TO THE LORD, THE ALMIGHTY

GT:    Full with Reeds 8', 4'
PED:  Full with Reed 16', Gt. to Ped.

*Erneuerten Gesangbuch*
**Arranged by Jerry Westenkuehler**

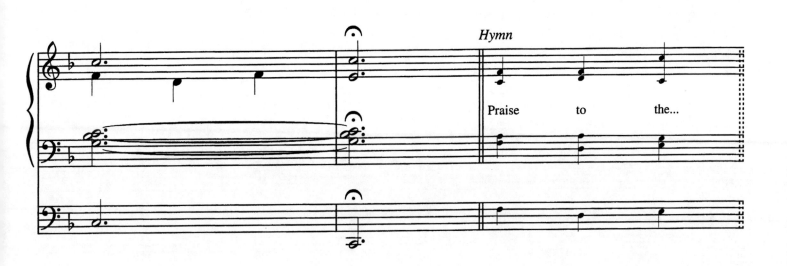

*Hymn*

Praise          to          the...

# REJOICE, YE PURE IN HEART

GT: Full
PED: Full

Arthur H. Messiter
Arranged by Jerry Westenkuehler

# REJOICE, YE PURE IN HEART

Arthur H. Messiter
Arranged by Mark Thewes

# SING PRAISE TO GOD WHO REIGNS ABOVE

GT: Full, no reeds
Ped: Full

*Kirchengesange*
**Arranged by Jerry Westenkuehler**

Sing    praise    to    God    who

# SING WE NOW OF CHRISTMAS

SW:   Full to Mixture
GT:   Full, Sw. to Gt.
PED: Full, Sw. to Ped.

Traditional French Carol
Arranged by Jerry Westenkuehler

# SILENT NIGHT HOLY NIGHT

SW: String Celeste 8'
GT: Flute 4', tremolo
PED: Soft 16', Sw. to Ped.

Franz Gruber
Arranged by Jerry Westenkuehler

Si - lent night, Ho - ly night...

# WE THREE KINGS OF ORIENT ARE

SW: Solo Reed
GT: Principals 8', 4', 2'
PED: 16', Gt. to Ped.

John H. Hopkins
**Arranged by Jerry Westenkuehler**

# WHAT CHILD IS THIS?

SW: ·Solo Reed
GT:  Full
PED: Full

16th Century English Melody
Arranged by Jerry Westenkuehler

# WHEN IN OUR MUSIC GOD IS GLORIFIED

**Traditional**
**Arranged by Mark Thewes**

# WHEN MORNING GILDS THE SKIES

Joseph Barbny
Arranged by Jerry Westenkuehler

GT: Full
PED: Full

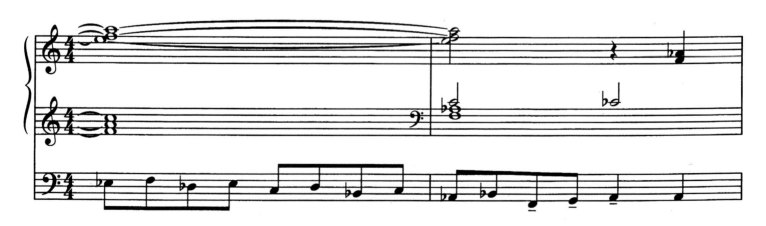